Under Pressure

Handling the Stresses of Keeping Up

Under Pressure

Handling the Stresses of Keeping Up

by Sari Earl and Stephanie Watson

Content Consultant
Dr. Robyn J. A. Silverman
Child/Teen Development Expert and Success Coach
Powerful Words Character Development

3 9063 10092 5786

Credits

Published by ABDO Publishing Company, 8000 West 78th Street, Edina, Minnesota 55439. Copyright © 2010 by Abdo Consulting Group, Inc. International copyrights reserved in all countries. No part of this book may be reproduced in any form without written permission from the publisher. The Essential Library™ is a trademark and logo of ABDO Publishing Company.

Printed in the United States.

Editor: Amy Van Zee
Copy Editor: Melissa Johnson
Interior Design and Production: Emily Love
Cover Design: Becky Daum

Library of Congress Cataloging-in-Publication Data
Earl, Sari.
  Under pressure : handling the stresses of keeping up / by Sari Earl & Stephanie Watson ; content consultant, Robyn J. A. Silverman.
    p. cm. — (Essential health : strong, beautiful girls)
  Includes index.
  ISBN 978-1-60453-755-0
  1. Stress in adolescence. 2. Stress management for teenagers. 3. Life skills. I. Watson, Stephanie, 1969- II. Title.

  BF724.3.S86U64 2010
  155.5'33—dc22
                              2009004415

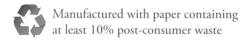

Manufactured with paper containing at least 10% post-consumer waste

Contents

Meet Dr. Robyn

Dr. Robyn Silverman loves to spend time with young people. It's what she does best! As a child and adolescent development specialist, Dr. Robyn has devoted her time to helping girls just like you become all they can be. Throughout the Strong, Beautiful Girls series, you'll hear her expert advice as she offers wisdom on boyfriends, school, and everything in between.

An award-winning body image expert and the creator of the Powerful Words Character System, Dr. Robyn likes to look on the bright side of life. She knows how tough it is to be a young woman in today's world, and she's prepared with encouragement to help you embrace your beauty even when your "frenemies" tell you otherwise. Dr. Robyn struggled with her own body image while growing up, so she knows what you're going through.

Dr. Robyn has been told she has a rare talent—to help girls share their wildest dreams and biggest problems. Her compassion makes her a trusted friend to many girls, and she considers it a gift to be able to interact with the young people who she sees as the leaders of tomorrow. She even started a girls' group, the Sassy Sisterhood Girls Circle, to help young women pinpoint how media messages impact their lives and body confidence so they can get healthy and get happy.

As a speaker and a success coach, her powerful messages have reached thousands of people. Her expert advice has been featured in *Prevention* magazine, *Parents* magazine, and the *Washington Post*. She was even a guest editor for the Dove Self-Esteem Fund: Campaign for Real Beauty. But she has an online presence too, and her writing can be found through her blogs, www.DrRobynsBlog.com and www.BodyImageBlog.com, or through her Web site, www.DrRobynSilverman.com. Dr. Robyn also enjoys spending time with her family in Massachusetts.

Dr. Robyn believes that young people are assets to be developed, not problems to be fixed. She's out to help you become the best you can be. As she puts it, "I'm stepping up to the plate to highlight news stories gone wrong, girls gone right, and programs that help to support strengths instead of weaknesses. I'd be grateful if you'd join me."

Take It from Us

Life is full of pressure, some of it good and some of it bad. Some sources of pressure are external, such as parents, teachers, friends, and society in general. But some sources of pressure are internal—the kind of pressure you put on yourself. Some pressure is productive, such as challenging yourself to improve your tennis serve or to finish a project you've started. Some pressure can make you feel bad about yourself, especially if it's applied in a negative way or if it pushes you to do something you don't want to do.

No matter the kind of pressure you're dealing with, too much of it can be harmful. It's like pumping air into a bicycle tire. If the tire is running low, you need to increase the air pressure so the bike rides well. But if there's too much air in the tire, at some point that tire may burst. You need to find a balance of motivation that's healthy for you.

Dealing with pressure is a skill that will help you for your entire life. It will help you figure out what challenges propel you to work harder and succeed. It will also help you recognize when that pressure is too much and you need to find ways to lessen it. Are your parents making too many demands on you? Do you feel stressed and overcommitted? Do your friends want you to act a certain way? Is your coach pushing you too hard? Knowing how to handle pressure can help you realize when your friends, parents, or teachers are coming down too hard on you and give you the skills to manage them.

We wrote this book with the hope that it will help you respond well to the normal pressures of everyday life and identify the pressures that can help motivate you. Additionally, we hope that you'll learn to identify harmful pressures and craft strategies for coping with them. Life is not meant to be a stress-free ride, but you can have strategies to deal with the bumps and potholes along the way.

XOXO,
Sari and Stephanie

1

The Pleaser

Your parents can be your greatest source of love and support in the world. At times, parents will pressure their daughter to do what they think is in her best interest. This kind of positive parental push can help motivate a child to work a little harder in school or to try out for a team instead of standing on the sidelines. Parents can sometimes see their daughter's potential when she doesn't yet realize what she's capable of.

Most parents want what's best for their children. But sometimes a child doesn't share her parents' idea of what's best for her. Listening to your parents' advice is key, but it's also important to follow your own passions and dreams.

You may feel as if one or both of your parents are pressuring you to think or act in a certain way. You may feel like one or both of your parents expect too much from you. You may even resent your parents' pressure. This can drive a wedge between you and the people who care most about you. Abby **You may feel like one or both of your parents expect too much from you.** was experiencing this problem. Read on to see how she learned that she needed to be honest with her overbearing mom.

Abby's Story

"Oh, look what's here!" Abby's mom cried, pulling a piece of paper from Abby's backpack.

Abby looked up from her math homework and turned to her mother. "What's here?"

"The application for the director to oversee the middle school musical!" her mother exclaimed. Abby looked back at her homework, not meeting her mother's eye. She'd been hoping that her mother wouldn't see the application and that the deadline would pass unnoticed. She didn't want to be director, but she knew that her mother wouldn't understand. "That sounds like a lot of work," Abby muttered.

"Not really. When I was director, I also played the lead in the show. It's fun!" Abby's mom smiled.

"After-school rehearsals, costumes . . . and the music. It was the highlight of the entire year." She picked up a pen and began writing on the form.

"What are you doing?" Abby asked, alarmed.

"I'm filling out the application for you," her mom answered.

Abby bit her lip, not wanting to disappoint her mother. "But . . . well, I was thinking about being in the show . . . " she started.

"Of course you'll be in the show! You're a Harding, and Hardings always direct the musical! There was me, your cousin Louisa, and both of your brothers."

Abby didn't say anything to her mom, but she was getting really worried. Abby was part of the math club at school, and it was one of her favorite activities. The Math Olympiad was in three weeks and her team was counting on her. Still, her mother seemed so excited, and Abby hated to disappoint her. Maybe she could fill out the application but wouldn't get picked as director.

Talk About It

- **Should Abby have told her mother that she didn't want to be the director?**

- **Do you think Abby should have shared her concerns about letting down her Math Olympiad team?**

- **How would you feel if your parent nominated you for a position you didn't want?**

A week later, Abby walked into Mr. Emmons's room, pulled her math club folder out of her backpack, and sat down at a desk. After studying the problem on the board, she began working through the computation.

Marlene stomped into the room. "What are you doing here?" she demanded.

"Yeah," Gina added, dropping her book loudly. "We don't like traitors in math club."

Frowning, Abby looked up. "What are you talking about?"

Marlene glared at Abby. "We heard about the musical. When were you going to tell us—the day

before the Olympiad? You know you can't do both. So what's it gonna be—us or them?"

Abby blinked in surprise. "I'm the director?"

Scowling, Marlene crossed her arms. "Like you didn't know!"

Abby shook her head, feeling overwhelmed. "But I don't want to be the director! My mom . . . she made me apply. I swear, I didn't think I was going to get it!"

"What did you expect?" Gina demanded. "Every member of your family has been director! But I thought you were going to help us win the Olympiad."

"But I want to win the Olympiad! I want to be on the team!" Abby insisted, trying to defend herself.

Just then, Mr. Emmons strode into the room, and he didn't look happy. "Math Olympiad is in two weeks, Abby, and your rehearsals start tomorrow. We'll be disqualified if we don't have a full team." He shook his head and sighed. "You know you're an asset to this team—and we are all counting on each other—but if you're going to be a member, we need you here with your head in the game."

"Math Olympiad is in two weeks, Abby, and your rehearsals start tomorrow. We'll be disqualified if we don't have a full team."

Talk About It

- **How do you think Abby feels? Have you ever felt this kind of pressure?**

- **Have you ever been in a situation where nothing seemed like the right answer?**

Abby knew what she wanted to do—to compete in the Math Olympiad. She didn't want to let her team or her teacher down. But how would her mother feel if she quit the musical? Abby was really conflicted. Still, she had made her decision. She went down to the choir room to talk to Mrs. Peskin.

"Mrs. Peskin? Can I talk to you about something?" Abby asked as she walked into the choir room.

"Of course!" Mrs. Peskin replied. "Are you here to talk about the musical? Rehearsals start tomorrow, you know."

"Yeah, well, that's what I wanted to talk to you about," Abby replied. "You see . . . um, I can't be the director."

"Oh," Mrs. Peskin said. "Is something wrong?"

"Well, my mom really wanted me to be the director. Both my brothers were directors . . ." Abby paused. "My mom filled out the application for me. I didn't want to disappoint her, but I really want to compete in the Math Olympiad. My team is counting on me."

Mrs. Peskin was disappointed to hear that Abby did not want to be director, but Abby was relieved that she had told Mrs. Peskin what she really wanted. Still, Abby was nervous to tell her mother the news.

Later that afternoon, Abby's mother drove up to the front of the school where Abby was waiting. With a knot in her stomach, Abby opened up the car door and slouched into the front seat. Her mom's face was tight with anger, and she didn't even say hello.

"Is there something you want to tell me, Abby?" her mom asked.

Looking away, Abby shrugged. "No."

"Really?"

Nervously, Abby shook her head.

Her mom's scowl deepened. "I called the principal today to discuss the fall fund-raiser, and guess what he told me?"

Shrugging, Abby swallowed.

"Principal Tipton told me you got the director position but then you told Mrs. Peskin that you didn't want it. Apparently you'd never wanted it. Your bossy, overbearing mother had pushed you into it."

Abby's heart seemed to skip a beat. She was mortified. "I didn't say that!" she exclaimed.

"Then what did you say, Abby? What did you tell Mrs. Peskin, who then told Principal Tipton, and probably half of the parent-teacher association?"

Talk About It

- Do you think that Abby should have discussed her decision with her mother before speaking to anyone at school? Why or why not?

- How do you think Abby's mother felt to hear the news from the principal, instead of from Abby?

Abby's mouth was dry as dust. "I just said that I wanted to do the Math Olympiad instead. I told Mrs. Peskin that I was on the math team." Abby's vision grew blurry, and she realized that she was crying. "And that I didn't really want to be director, but I didn't want to disappoint you."

Abby's mom shook her head, her voice filled with pain and anger. "Why didn't you tell me you didn't want to be director?"

"I thought you'd be mad at me," Abby answered. Her shoulders were shaking and tears were rolling down her cheeks.

"But it's your decision! I'm sorry that I didn't ask you before I filled out the application. I just thought you would want to follow in the family footsteps," Abby's mom said. "But when you told people that I made you do it, you made me seem like a terrible mother. I didn't realize you felt so pressured."

Abby lowered her head. She felt awful.

Abby's mom sighed. "Now instead of disappointing me, you've embarrassed me, but even more, I'm hurt."

Abby looked up. "Hurt?"

Her mom nodded. "I'm hurt that you didn't feel you could be honest with me. You could've told me. I'm your mother, and I want what's best for you."

Leaning over, Abby's mom wrapped her arm around her daughter and hugged her close. "It's not about doing a certain thing, Abby. It's about being the best you can be at whatever *you* choose to do. I know I pushed you in a certain direction, and I'm sorry. But in the future, can you please be honest with me?"

Sobbing, Abby felt like she wanted to crawl into a hole and die. She had been so afraid that her mother wouldn't love her if she weren't exactly who her mother wanted her to be. But in her fear, she'd hurt the person she loved most. And the worst part was that she could have avoided the entire situation if only she'd been honest at the very beginning.

Talk About It

- Have you ever been afraid to tell the truth for fear of how someone might react?

- What do you think Abby will learn from this experience?

Ask Dr. Robyn

Abby was so focused on pleasing her mother that she was scared to tell her how she really felt. In doing so, she made it seem as if her mother was pressuring Abby to do something against her will. This hurt and upset her mother, and it made Abby feel even worse as she realized that the entire situation could have been avoided if she had just been honest.

A lot of kids don't want to tell their parents the truth because they're afraid of how their parents might react. They want to please their parents and not disappoint them. Other kids feel so much pressure that they choose to rebel. Neither of these responses is healthy, and they can lead to feeling disappointed, frustrated, and disconnected from the people you love. If you're feeling pressured by your parents, talk with them about it. Do it respectfully and try to listen to the reasoning behind their demands. Keep the lines of communication open with your parents. It will help you feel more comfortable talking to them, even about difficult subjects.

Get Healthy

1. It's hard to be candid with someone else if you're not clear on what you want yourself. Figure out what you want and the best way to communicate it so that you can be straightforward with your parents.

2. If you're uncomfortable speaking with your parents about the pressure you feel from them, try to find a confidant, such as a school counselor or therapist, who can give you good advice for approaching your parents.

3. Try to remember that your parents are people too. Their feelings can be hurt by things you say or do.

4. Be a good listener. By listening well, you can get a better sense of people instead of rushing to judgment on how they might feel or what they might expect.

The Last Word from Sari

Even though it can be difficult, try to keep in mind that your parents really do want what's best for you. They can pressure you to progress in a positive way, such as pushing you to pedal harder that first time you ride a bike. Yet even if they mean well, parents can sometimes make too many demands on their children. Start communicating with your parents and let them know that you need to lessen the pressure. Ask for their support so you can work out a resolution together. If that doesn't work, find a trustworthy adult, such as a school counselor or a relative, to help you decrease the pressure you're feeling.

2

Poor Little Poor Girl

Every school has at least one clique of girls who are pretty, popular, and virtually untouchable. They wear the latest fashions, date the cutest boys, and are worshipped by everyone else in the school. But that isn't always a good thing.

If you're on the outside looking into one of these cliques, you might feel desperately jealous of these popular girls. Even if you're in the middle of the group, it can be difficult to constantly live up to your friends' pressure and high expectations. You may feel as though you have to look and act like everyone else in your group. When all of your friends are wearing the latest designer jeans, it's natural for you to want to do the same, even if you can't afford those jeans. This can cause jealousy, discontent, and frustration.

When all of your friends are wearing the latest designer jeans, it's natural for you to want to do the same, even if you can't afford those jeans.

Hailey felt like an outcast because she didn't have enough money to dress like all her friends. She thought that having money and nice clothes equaled happiness, but she learned that was far from the truth.

Hailey's Story

"Did you see the way Jared was smiling at you in gym today?" Izzy whispered.

"Really? He's so cute!" Hailey gushed. They were sitting outside and eating lunch on the wide green lawn behind their private school.

"I think he likes you," said Izzy. "You should ask him to the dance on Saturday."

Hailey was hesitant. "Um, maybe I will."

"I saw this really hot dress at the mall that would look great on you," Izzy continued. "You should definitely buy it."

Hailey really wanted to go to the Fall Festival Dance, and she wanted to go with Jared even more.

But there was no way she was going to be able to afford a dress from the mall. There was also no way she was wearing the thrift-store dress that she'd already worn five times. She'd be humiliated!

She looked at Izzy. Izzy was wearing diamond stud earrings, a cashmere sweater, and really expensive jeans. Her friend looked like she had just walked out of a fashion magazine. Then Hailey checked her own inventory: a blue polyester tunic that her mother had bought on clearance and a pair of last year's designer jeans that Hailey had found crumpled on the dressing room floor at a discount outlet. It was so unfair!

Talk About It

- **Have you ever turned down going to a social event because you felt as if you didn't have anything to wear?**

- **Have you ever felt jealous of something your friend had? Why?**

- **What kind of influence do your friends have over how you dress and act?**

After school, Hailey walked three blocks to Oak Park, where her mother picked her up. She never let her mother drive up in front of the school. She'd be so embarrassed if any of her friends saw her mom's

old beat-up station wagon. All of their mothers drove brand-new luxury cars.

"Hi, Sweetie. Did you have a good day?" her mom asked as Hailey got in the car and slammed the door. Hailey mumbled something inaudible.

"What's got you so upset? Did something happen at school?" her mom asked. Hailey just glared out the window. "I can't help you if you don't talk to me," her mother pressed.

"You want to know why I'm upset?" Hailey turned to her mother angrily. "I am so sick of watching my friends get everything they want! They all get expensive clothes! They all get to go skiing in Aspen every winter break! I hate being poor!"

"Oh, Hailey," her mom sighed. "I know it's tough being the only scholarship student at a private school. I'm trying to earn enough money to get you the things you want, but it's not easy to do on my own."

"Well maybe if you and dad hadn't split up, we'd still be living in a nice house, and we wouldn't have to buy everything on clearance!" Hailey accused.

Her mother looked stricken. "Hailey, that's not fair. I'm doing the best I can for you. I'm working two jobs just to keep us in our apartment." Although Hailey felt bad that she'd hurt her mother, she didn't say anything.

Talk About It

- How do you think Hailey's mother felt when Hailey complained about their financial situation?

- Have you ever yelled at your parents because they weren't giving you what you wanted? How did they react? How did it make you feel?

On Saturday, Hailey's mother took her out for lunch at a local diner, and then they went shopping for a new dress at the mall. Jared had actually asked *her* to the dance! The hard part was trying to find a dress that looked nice on her mother's shoestring budget.

As they were making their way toward the discount store, Hailey spotted Izzy out of the corner of her eye. Oh no, she thought. Please don't let her see me going into the bargain basement!

But Izzy didn't see her. She was too focused on her own mother, who was loudly berating her in the middle of the mall. "I swear, Izzy! How could you sit there and eat an entire ice cream sundae?" Mrs. Fisher's diamond-ringed hands waved wildly in the air as she yelled at her daughter. "Do you think you're going to fit into that $400 dress I bought you? Look, your hips are swelling already."

Hailey didn't want to eavesdrop, but she couldn't help it. Everybody was turning around to look at Izzy and her mother. "I'm going to the jewelry store. Meet me in the parking lot in an hour. And don't be late! I'm meeting my trainer at 6:00, and then I have dinner reservations!" Mrs. Fisher yelled and walked away, leaving Izzy standing alone, looking mortified.

When Hailey walked up to her, Izzy had tears in her eyes. "I'm so embarrassed that you saw that," she whispered. "My mom can be such a witch sometimes."

When Hailey walked up to her, Izzy had tears in her eyes.

Hailey looked over at her own mom, who was waiting patiently for her by the food court. Her mom was not rich, but she was loving and kind, and that meant a lot more than any designer outfit, Hailey thought.

Talk About It

- Who do you think really has it better—Izzy or Hailey? Why?

- If given the choice between being rich and having a really supportive family, which would you choose? Why?

Ask Dr. Robyn

Girls often set impossibly high standards for themselves. They feel as if they have to be perfect in every way. They have to wear the right clothes in just the right colors and styles—clothes that are often incredibly expensive.

The media only adds to these pressures. Girls on television and in the movies are professionally styled to look gorgeous, even if they are just wearing sweats and have their hair in a ponytail. Girls in the real world try to emulate what they see in the media, but not everyone can afford expensive clothes and accessories. Those who don't achieve just the right look may feel like losers or failures.

Instead of letting your clothes define who you are, develop your own sense of style. You'll be surprised at how much your friends will respect you for it. Surround yourself with people who value friendship more than money and expensive clothes. The popular but self-absorbed girls might be fun to hang out with today, but the real friends are the ones who will stick with you no matter what you look like or how much money you have.

Get Healthy

1. Money and popularity don't necessarily equal happiness. Remember that even the

richest, most popular girls at school have their issues—no one is perfect.

2. Rather than following the crowd, follow your own passions. Whether you're a great art- ist, musician, or writer, focus on what you do best.

3. You don't need to spend a fortune to look great. Make the most out of what you have. A cool necklace or belt can add style to even the most basic wardrobe.

4. If there's an article of clothing you absolutely must have, get an after-school job (such as babysitting) and earn the money to buy it. It will mean so much more to you if you pay for it yourself.

The Last Word from Stephanie

Fashion can be really fun, but if you dwell too much on dressing like everyone else, you'll just be one of the crowd. Recently I spotted a teen- age girl with the most unique style I've ever seen. Instead of following popular fashion, she had created her own look by combining vintage and modern clothing. I wish I'd had the guts to be as daring as her when I was in school. My point is, don't waste time trying to look like everyone else. Find your own style and be proud of it!

3

The Team Loser

Exercise is a great way to stay in shape, feel good, improve your strength, and live a longer, healthier life. It also can help girls feel better about their bodies and themselves. Exercising can be done alone in sports such as running and horseback riding, or with others in organized sports such as soccer and basketball. Working out with friends can be a great way to stay healthy and socialize, too. Exercising with others can be like working toward a common goal. It can be inspiring and rewarding.

Being on a team can help enhance a girl's discipline or help her develop leadership and teamwork skills. Teammates can encourage and support each other to go the extra mile or achieve a new goal. In Samantha's case, however, her teammates were anything but encouraging. Keep reading to learn how she dealt with the pressure of difficult teammates and conquered the obstacles holding her back.

Being on a team can help enhance a girl's discipline or help her develop leadership and teamwork skills.

Samantha's Story

Samantha shifted her bag on her shoulder and dropped her soccer ball to the ground. She was dreading soccer practice. Actually, she liked the drills and loved the sport. But it was her teammates, Lillian, Kendra, and Francine, who made practice miserable for Samantha. She even called them "The Three Furies," but only in her head.

It would've been easy to dismiss these girls if they weren't so good at soccer. But they were the best players on the team. Lillian and Francine were forwards, and Kendra was the goalkeeper. Kendra was good, but she had been having a rough season. The team hadn't won a game yet, and that made the Three Furies particularly mean.

Samantha's feet dragged as she moved onto the field. Francine and Kendra were passing a ball back and forth between them while Lillian kicked into the goal. Samantha's heart sank as she realized that the rest of the team hadn't shown up yet and Coach Gates was nowhere to be seen.

Kendra looked up and set her foot on the ball, stopping it short. "Haven't you quit yet, Slowpoke Sam?"

"Yeah, Slowpoke Sam." Francine set her hands on her hips. "Don't you have a nap to take?"

Talk About It

- Do you play a team sport? If so, does your team work well together, or are your teammates competitive with each other?

- Have you ever felt pressure from a coach to succeed?

- Has anyone ever made fun of the way you played a sport? If so, how did you react?

It killed Samantha that her teammates thought she was a loser who dragged down the team. She loved soccer and lived for every moment she had on the field, even though Coach Gates kept her on the sidelines more than any other player on the team. Coach Gates thought the Three Furies were faultless, and he kept them in the game as much as possible. Francine and Kendra were his favorites, and he said

they were being "good leaders" when they harassed the other girls on the team. When Samantha complained once about Kendra being mean, Coach Gates told her that she needed to be a team player or quit. Samantha's mother wanted her to stop playing, too. She said the games were painful to watch. Sometimes Samantha wondered why she continued trying so hard when it seemed like such an uphill battle.

Just then, the rest of the team came onto the field. They were followed by Mr. Hartz, the eighth-grade French teacher. Mr. Hartz was wearing a coach's uniform. Stepping forward, he spoke to the team. "I'm Coach Hartz. Coach Gates has had a family emergency. Everything looks as if it will be all right, but I'll be your coach for the rest of the season."

The Three Furies groaned and made faces. The coach glared at them until they looked away, pretending that they hadn't done anything wrong.

Coach Hartz continued, "I know a few of you, but not all. So please tell me your name and what position you play." He looked at Samantha. "How about you get us started?"

Samantha exhaled. "My name's Samantha, I play offense—"

"You mean offensively," Kendra sneered.

Talk About It

- **Have you ever felt defeated about something you were doing? Did you give up, or keep trying?**
- **Do you think that her teammates' taunts made Samantha try harder or simply feel bad about herself?**

Coach Hartz turned to Kendra. "That'll be four laps on the track for you. We never, ever say a word about our teammates unless it's in support or encouragement. And consider yourself warned. If I hear a mean comment from anyone else, they'll sit on the sidelines for the next game."

During practice that day, Samantha worked really hard, trying to show Coach Hartz that she was worthy of being on the team. Still, during the scrimmage she was outmaneuvered the entire time. I'm too slow! she worried.

When Coach Hartz motioned to speak with Samantha, her heart sank. He's going to take me out, I just know it! she thought. But Coach Hartz surprised her by saying, "You're a good passer and anticipate the ball well, Samantha. Have you ever considered playing defense?"

When Coach Hartz motioned to speak with Samantha, her heart sank.

Samantha shook her head. "No. Since I was little I always played on offense."

Coach Hartz smiled. "Why don't you try it? Kendra seems to need the help. Play sweeper."

Talk About It

- What do you think of Coach Hartz's coaching style? Do you think it will help the team be more successful?

- Have you ever had to play a new role on a team or in a club? How did it feel to switch to something new?

Samantha switched positions on the field, trying to ignore the weird stares she got from the Three Furies. During the next scrimmage, Samantha played defense. The first time the ball came near her, she stopped it from approaching the goal by kicking it out of bounds. It felt strange playing a different position, but it wasn't bad. The next time the ball came at her, Samantha passed it to Lillian, who took it down the field and scored. Lillian turned and stared at Samantha as if she'd never seen her before.

Beaming, Coach Hartz clapped his hands. "Now that's what I'm talking about! You're a natural sweeper if I've ever seen one, Samantha! If you work at it, the other team will have a hard time getting anything past you!"

The rest of the season, Samantha worked harder than she'd ever trained in her life. She realized that she loved playing defense. She'd watch the ball and figure out the best position to be in to stop any goals. Kendra started thanking her after saves. Her teammates, including Francine, would pat her on the back and say, "great play." Lillian started drilling with her so they could work on their passing. Samantha's mom started coming to more games and cheering her on. At the end of the season, her teammates got together and gave Samantha a broom with a certificate pasted on it that read, *To Samantha, The Super Clean Queen, The Best Sweeper Ever.*

Talk About It

- Have you ever felt as if you were in the right sport, but the wrong position? What did you do about it?

- How do you think the team's changes made Samantha feel about playing soccer?

Great teamwork is like a talented orchestra. Different members bring diverse sounds together, work in harmony, and can create beautiful music. Each player on a team has something valuable to contribute, and players must work together to be successful. It's natural to feel competitive. Yet the healthiest form of competition drives you to be *your* best— that's what's in your power. You can't control how well someone else plays or how tall they are or how much training they do. But you can work to be your best and contribute to the team effort. If you love a sport but you don't feel you're playing well, try another position. Like Sam, you might find that you'll help the team even more if you try a different role.

Being part of a group can help you learn to appreciate others for what they have to offer and create worthwhile relationships in settings other than school. And if you are a leader on a team, it is extra important to say encouraging things to your teammates. It's no fun to play on a team with mean people. So remember to encourage, not tear down.

Get Healthy

1. If you're on a team, respect the coach and your teammates. Show up on time and always try your hardest. Show good

sportsmanship with teammates and with the opposing team.

2. If you see a teammate struggling, help her. Offer to practice extra with her or train with her in the weight room after practice. It can be a great way to develop your own game and improve the team's dynamics.

3. Exercise is an excellent way to relieve stress, but if being on a team significantly increases your stress, consider changing to a different sport or activity.

The Last Word from Sari

When I was in high school, I played doubles on the tennis team. We lost consistently. Then I got a new partner named Callie. She was younger than me, and I worried that she wouldn't be as good as my last partner. Callie and I turned out to be a great team. She made me recognize that my other partner had been a ball hog and had been so competitive that she threw off my game. Callie wasn't trying to show me up, but instead worked with me to improve our team's game. We had a lot of fun at practices, and matches didn't seem quite as intense. We played great together and made it to the finals. I realized it was because I had a real partner who worked with me to win. Callie reminded me that winning is great, but enjoying the game is the real key to success.

4

The Wannabe

Open up any celebrity magazine and you'll see pages and pages of girls not much older than you. They'll all be rail thin, impossibly beautiful, and dressed in the most expensive designer clothes.

Read on, and you might learn about the role one of these ladies has just landed on the hottest nighttime drama. She'll be getting paid thousands of dollars for every single episode. With that money, she plans to splurge on spa treatments and shopping sprees at the most exclusive boutiques.

Perfect life, right? A lot of girls think so. They are so in love with the idea of fame, wealth, and beauty that they try to model themselves after the people they see on the screen. This puts a lot of pressure on girls to look and act a certain way. But what they don't realize is that the celebrity magazines and television shows only reveal part of

Open up any celebrity magazine and you'll see pages and pages of girls not much older than you. They'll all be rail thin, impossibly beautiful, and dressed in the most expensive designer clothes.

the story. In reality, a lot of famous people have big problems. Tia would have done anything to trade places with her favorite actress, until she discovered that the reality didn't live up to the hype.

Tia's Story

Tia had wanted to become an actress since she was a little girl. When she was young, she loved to dress up like her favorite actresses and act out scenes from movies. Lately, Tia had been bugging her mom to take her to auditions and local casting calls, hoping to catch her lucky break. The casting directors told her that successful actresses needed to have a certain "look." Tia knew exactly what look they were talking about—she had seen tons of pictures of thin, glamorous actresses in the celebrity magazines she read.

Tia's favorite actress was Laila Jameson. In fact, Tia had become obsessed with copying Laila's style, and she followed all the latest celebrity gossip about Laila's television show and personal life. Tia thought that if she could just look and act like Laila Jameson, she was sure to break into show business. So she poured all her energy into doing just that.

Talk About It

- **Do you think Tia's obsession with Laila Jameson is healthy? Why or why not?**

- **Have you ever felt as if you had to look or act a certain way to get something you really wanted? What happened?**

Tia never missed an episode of Laila's television show. She avoided hanging out with friends on nights when the show was on so that she wouldn't have to miss it. One night, her parents came home late from work, so they ate dinner later than usual. By the time they sat down to eat, Tia was nervous that she would miss the first few minutes of the show. She started shoveling her dinner into her mouth as fast as she could.

"Tia, slow down! You'll give yourself indigestion." Her mother looked at her disapprovingly.

"No time, Mom," Tia mumbled through a mouthful of potatoes. She gulped it down with a big chug of milk. "*Huntington Beach* is on in five minutes, and Whitney's about to find out if Billy cheated on her!"

Her parents didn't have time to protest as Tia put her dishes in the sink and ran upstairs to her room. She switched on the television and flopped down on her bed underneath the giant poster of Laila Jameson. It was the one where Laila was wearing the black mini-dress. She looked so pretty and skinny in it! Tia was planning to buy the same outfit—just as soon as she lost 15 pounds.

Talk About It

- Do you think Tia is too caught up in her favorite show and her favorite actress? Why or why not?

- Is there any celebrity you admire, or are even obsessed with? What do you like about him or her?

The next morning, Tia threw on her "Save the Polar Bears" T-shirt (it was Laila's favorite cause) and ran downstairs for breakfast. But she brushed aside her mother's offer of cereal and toast. "No carbs for me, Mom. Remember what the casting director said about having a certain look? I have that big audition coming up in a few weeks, so I'm trying to lose weight. I'm sticking to blue and purple foods.

"No carbs for me, Mom. Remember what the casting director said about having a certain look?"

Laila lost ten pounds that way." Tia scooped some blueberries and blackberries into a bowl.

"Honestly, Tia. You're going to be starving. You have to eat something more substantial than berries," her mother protested.

"Mom, it's fine," Tia countered. "Laila told *Celebrity Dish* magazine she didn't feel hungry at all on this diet, and she was on it for a whole month. I want to get down to a size 0, just like her! Then maybe I'll land a leading role."

"If Laila Jameson jumped off a bridge, would you jump too?" her mom asked.

"Don't be so dramatic, Mom," Tia said as she rolled her eyes. "Berries are very good for you."

By lunchtime, Tia was starving. Still, she was determined to stick to her diet. She opened her container of steamed eggplant and purple potatoes.

"Yuck! Are you going to eat that?" Across the lunch table her best friend Rachel looked disgusted.

"Sure. Laila loves this," Tia said, but she looked longingly at Rachel's slice of cheese pizza.

Talk About It

- **Do you think that following Laila Jameson's diet might be risky for Tia? If so, why?**

- **Do you think it is worth it for Tia to change who she is to get an acting job? Why or why not?**

"Oh, I almost forgot to tell you!" Rachel put down her pizza. "There was this crazy article about Laila Jameson in this month's issue of *Hot Stars* magazine." She reached into her book bag and pulled out the magazine, which was covered in pictures of the hottest young actors and actresses.

Tia nearly jumped across the table trying to grab the magazine. "Well, what did it say?" she asked.

"Hold on, I'm getting to it." Rachel thumbed through the pages. "Here it is! It seems your favorite actress was caught stealing a handbag from some swanky boutique."

Tia's mouth dropped. Laila Jameson? Shoplifting? It didn't make any sense. "That can't be," she said, shaking her head. "She has a ton of money. Why would she need to steal?"

"Says here she's got a little kleptomania problem," her friend replied. "Apparently she likes to steal for the thrill of it."

Tia was in shock. And it was about to get worse.

"And get this," Rachel continued. "When a police officer arrested her, she took a swing at him and called him a racist name." She looked up from her magazine, frowning. "Not cool."

Tia's hero—her idol—was a thief, and worse, she was racist! Tia felt like she was going to burst into tears. She roughly pushed away her container of purple vegetables. "Let's talk about this after I get a slice of pizza!"

Talk About It

- How do you think Tia felt when she discovered that her hero wasn't the perfect person Tia thought she was? Do you think Tia will still want to become an actress?

- Have you ever idolized someone, only to find out they weren't as wonderful as you'd imagined?

- Are you a role model to anyone? What qualities do you think a good role model should have?

Ask Dr. Robyn

Tia wanted to become an actress, so she looked to celebrities for rules on how she should look or act. She felt pressure to have a certain appearance to land an acting role, but that pressure pushed her into some unhealthy activities, such as strange diets and avoiding friends to watch television. Reading about Laila's arrest was the wake-up call she needed. It helped her see that maybe the glamorous life she wanted wasn't really so glamorous after all.

Celebrity culture puts a lot of pressure on stars to have a certain appearance, and this pressure can bring serious consequences. That model who wears a size 0 may be literally starving herself to get that way. Everyone has their problems, and that includes celebrities.

Rather than looking for celebrities to idolize, look to the people who inspire you every day—such as the art teacher who first recognized your talent, the parent who taught you to ride a bike, or the friend who stuck with you through all the hard times. They are your real heroes.

Get Healthy

1. Don't use the waiflike models you see walking the runway as your body inspiration.

The only ideal body is a healthy one, and the only way to get healthy is to eat a well-balanced diet and get plenty of exercise.

2. Try not to compare yourself to others. You have your own talents. Recognize and be proud of them.

3. Make a list of all the things you love about your own life. Take out that list and look at it whenever you're feeling like someone else has it better than you.

4. Remember that even the most beautiful, rich, and famous girls have their issues. They have to constantly live in the public eye, and they often are judged by their appearance. It's not easy for anyone to live up to those standards.

The Last Word from Stephanie

It's okay to like celebrities, but find role models who inspire you to be the best person you can be. Look around—your real hero could be right in front of you. When I was younger, I liked all the famous pop singers. I went to their concerts and put up their posters all over my room. But looking back, I realized that the guy I really should have been idolizing was my dad. He was the one who showed me how to plant a garden and taught me to love ballet. He was there for me every single day. He was a real friend and a real hero.

5

The Victim

*A*dolescence may be a time when a girl feels all sorts of emotions—sometimes one right after the other! Feeling anger is normal. There are healthy ways to express it, such as talking through the problem, walking away from a frustrating incident, thinking calm thoughts, or going to a trustworthy adult for help. It's important for a girl to understand that she has choices in how to respond when she's angry or in a difficult situation. A girl can seek help if she cannot control her anger. Likewise, she can ask for help if she is the victim of bullying.

Studies have shown that bullies are often victims of aggressive behaviors themselves. Children with bullying behaviors often come from families in which there is anger, harsh discipline, or inconsistent parenting. These children don't learn the skills necessary to deal with anger or conflict in a healthy way, and their pent-up emotions can come out in the form of picking on others. Bullying can also reflect insecurities or a sense of isolation. These facts don't excuse bullying behavior, nor do they make it any easier on the person suffering from the bullying. No matter the

Children with bullying behaviors often come from families in which there is anger, harsh discipline, or inconsistent parenting.

cause of the bullying, it has to be stopped. In Emma's case, she didn't care what made her bully so mean; she just wanted her to go away.

Emma's Story

Emma's heart was hammering as she headed to her locker. It was second period, which was the time her enemy, Jackie Henderson, liked to hang out on the second floor of the school. Emma's steps slowed. The choice between being late for science class and encountering Jackie was a no-brainer. Emma did everything she could to avoid the meanest girl in seventh grade.

Jackie had been picking on Emma since the start of the year, having decided for some reason that Emma deserved humiliation. Emma didn't know what she'd

done to invite this horrible attention, but it had made seventh grade miserable. Emma felt like everything she did was either to avoid or to pacify Jackie. She spent more time thinking about Jackie than anyone else in the world. She even drew pictures of Jackie in her notebook and crossed them out.

Biting her lip, Emma peeked down the hall. Whew! No enemy in sight, she thought. Quickly she walked down the hallway. Just as Emma was about to reach her locker, Jackie stepped out of a nearby classroom.

Jackie was tall and broad, with the body of a line-backer. She crossed her arms and sneered. "String Bean Emma! What do you eat for breakfast, skinny pills?" She stepped over to Emma's locker and stood in front of it as if daring Emma to try to get past her. "Where do you think you're going?"

Talk About It

- Do you think that blocking Emma's locker is a form of bullying? What would you do if a big, tough girl blocked your way?

- Do you think it is healthy that Emma spends so much time worrying about Jackie? Should she do anything to try to stop the bullying?

- If you were Emma, how would you feel about being teased about your body?

Just then, a crowd of girls came out of a nearby classroom. Everyone saw Jackie blocking Emma's locker and stopped to watch. A few of the girls looked at Emma sympathetically, but clearly they were too afraid to interfere.

Emma tried to step around Jackie, but Jackie moved in front of her.

Everyone saw Jackie blocking Emma's locker and stopped to watch. A few of the girls looked at Emma sympathetically, but clearly they were too afraid to interfere.

Emma felt her cheeks burn. Hate and embarrassment filled her so powerfully that she wanted to cry.

Monica, a seventh grader who was also captain of the soccer team, shifted her books in her arms and exclaimed, "Come on, Jackie, let her get to her locker."

Jackie glared at Monica. "What's it to you?" Then after a moment, she stepped aside. "Fine, I was going to anyway. I'm just foolin' around. Right, Emma?"

Emma knew everyone was watching her as she opened her locker. Then suddenly, Jackie reached into her locker and grabbed her blue bag. Emma turned, yelling, "Hey!"

Jackie waved Emma's blue bag like it was a flag. "What's this, String Bean? Your stash of diet pills?"

Now a group of seventh- and eighth-grade boys joined the crowd. Emma grabbed for her bag, but Jackie pushed her away. Jackie unzipped the blue bag and pulled out a tampon. "Ooh," Jackie jeered. "Emma's got her period!"

At that moment, Emma wished she were dead.

Talk About It

- **Have you ever been picked on or teased? How did it make you feel?**

- **Have you ever stood up for someone else the way Monica did for Emma? Why do you think she did that?**

- **Has anyone ever stood up for you? If so, how did it make you feel?**

Word of the tampon incident raced around the school faster than lightning. Then matters got worse when Principal Benton heard what happened. He called Emma into his office and made her share all the mortifying details. Next he interviewed Monica, a bunch of seventh-grade boys who had been in the hallway, and finally Jackie. As Emma watched the parade of witnesses, she was so miserable that she borrowed a friend's cell phone, called her mom, and begged to go home. But she wouldn't tell her mother why, so her mother said she had to wait until the end of the day. That meant three more hours of embarrassment. Emma escaped to the library, where it was quiet. She sat on the floor feeling defeated.

Anna, a seventh grader with multicolored braces, ran up to Emma. "Emma! Principal Benton suspended Jackie for the rest of the week! He even called her parents! Her mom's here, and she's got to take Jackie home now, before the end of school!"

Talk About It

- Why do you think Emma didn't tell her mother what had happened with Jackie?

- Do you think that Emma should have discussed the bullying with Principal Benton or one of the teachers before the tampon incident?

- How do you think Emma feels about Jackie's suspension?

A crowd of excited seventh graders had gathered by the window. Standing, Emma joined the group, wondering what they were watching. It was Jackie and her mom, heading toward the parking lot. Jackie's mom was pulling Jackie by the arm as Jackie cried in pain.

Jackie's mom pushed her daughter against the car with a loud bang. A hush fell over the seventh graders as they watched Jackie's mom open the door and shove Jackie into the front seat. Jackie saw the seventh graders watching from the window and slouched deep in her seat, her face filled with shame. The students couldn't hear what Jackie's mom was saying to her, but she was yelling and waving her arms. It was clear that she was angry. Jackie kept crying and avoided looking back at the school.

"Wow," Emma murmured, horrified. "Her mom's *so* mean."

Monica shook her head sadly. "You should see her father."

Emma was surprised at how she felt. "I actually feel sorry for her," she told Monica. She realized that she couldn't think of Jackie as her enemy anymore. "I hope she'll be all right."

Talk About It

- How do you feel about the way Jackie's mom treated her? Does that treatment make it okay for Jackie to be a bully? Why or why not?

- Why didn't Emma think of Jackie as an enemy after she saw the incident in the parking lot?

- Do you have any suggestions for how Emma can deal with Jackie after she comes back from suspension?

Ask Dr. Robyn

Bullying behaviors can take on a number of different forms, some subtler than others. These actions can be verbal, such as taunts, threats, harassment, spreading rumors, teasing, or intimidation. Bullying can take physical forms such as hitting, slapping, pushing, shoving, or starting fights. Bullying can also be emotional. Girls can be bullied emotionally when another person intentionally isolates them, spreads rumors about them, or constantly lies to them. Even though it's not physical, emotional bullying is still bullying.

One of the biggest fears that victims of bullying have is that their concerns will be ignored or laughed at by an adult. No matter what bullying you witness or suffer, it's important to break the silence. Speak up if you feel uncomfortable with a situation. If you tell an adult and he or she doesn't take you seriously, tell another one. It's important to find someone who will listen and help.

Friends can also help. If you feel victimized, strengthen your existing friendships or make new ones to make sure you don't feel isolated. Seek ways to be with your friends when you feel victimized by others. And of course, you can do things to help yourself. You can also find ways to improve your conflict resolution skills or assertiveness skills through reading books on bullying or taking a class on physical and nonphysical self-defense. Be aware of your posture and how you carry yourself. This can let others know that you are confident and sure of yourself.

Get Healthy

1. Find out if your school has an official policy on bullying. If your school doesn't have an anti-bullying policy, see if you can get your parents, teachers, or counselor to help establish one.

2. Ask your counselor to make a confidential drop box where students can safely deposit notes describing any bullying incidents they witness.

3. Engage in physical activities that give you confidence and a strong sense of self-worth, such as martial arts or team sports.

The Last Word from Sari

Being the victim of bullying can feel really lonely. It can feel as if everyone hates you, especially when nobody will stand up for you. Every school has bullies. Look for the more subtle signs of bullying, and don't be afraid to speak up for yourself and for others. You should never have to suffer abuse in silence.

6

The Athlete

Professional athletes constantly take their bodies to the edge. They train for hours each day because they know that each competition or game puts their reputation on the line, and they'll reap big rewards if they win.

Although they don't usually collect a big paycheck or get high-paid commercial endorsements like the pros, young athletes also face great pressure to win—pressure from their coaches, their teammates, and their parents. Some parents put pressure on their children to win college scholarships to help pay for college. Some coaches put pressure on their players to lose or gain weight to help their team win competitions. Failure can be devastating to a young athlete's family, their team, and their self-esteem.

Playing a sport is great for you—it helps keep your body in shape and gives you a healthy sense of competition and sportsmanship. But when that sport starts to take over your life by stealing time away from school, friends, and family, you're probably overdoing it. For Wendy, gymnastics was becoming an overwhelming and increasingly dangerous activity, and it was time for her to do something about it.

Playing a sport is great for you—it helps keep your body in shape and gives you a healthy sense of competition and sportsmanship.

Wendy's Story

"Joely, point your toes on that back handspring! Laura, keep your body tight on the next vault! Jennifer, that landing was way too wobbly." Coach Jones stood in the middle of the mat, simultaneously shouting directions to the handful of gymnasts who were practicing on the floor exercise, vault, uneven bars, and balance beam.

Wendy had so far been spared her coach's criticism. She was working on her dismount off the balance beam. She was pretty good at it already, but she was determined to get her tuck just perfect. She practiced over and over again, even though the blisters on her fingers were killing her.

"Not bad, Wendy." Coach Jones walked over and nodded approvingly as Wendy completed her twenty-sixth dismount in a row. "But . . . " She pointed to Wendy's flat stomach. "Better watch the sweets this week. You don't want that belly to get in the way of your routine." She walked away, headed for Wendy's teammate Liza, who was practicing on the uneven bars.

Wendy looked down at her stomach. It did look big. It must have been those three apples she ate last night. She'd have to cut back on her eating—a lot. Wendy jumped back up on the balance beam to try her dismount again.

Talk About It

- **Do you think Wendy is working too hard at her sport? Do you think working too hard may have consequences?**

- **Do you play a sport? How often do you practice? Do you feel pressure to do well?**

- **Was Coach Jones being too tough on Wendy? What effect might the weight comment have on Wendy's self-esteem?**

Gymnastics practice ran until 8:00 p.m. that night. At 10:00 p.m., Wendy crashed into bed. She was so exhausted that she slept right through her alarm clock the next morning. A loud knock at her bedroom door woke her up. "Wendy, you need to get up," her mother yelled through the door. "Remember that you have practice at 12:30."

Wendy's eyes cracked open, slowly focusing on the shelf of trophies and ribbons above her bureau. Then her eyes shifted down to her digital clock. 11:55 a.m. Oh no! She jumped out of bed and out the

door, rushing past her mother into the bathroom. She could hear the phone ringing in her room, but there was no time to answer it.

A few seconds later her mother yelled through the bathroom door. "Cassie's on the phone!" Wendy popped open the door with her toothbrush in her mouth. Her mother covered the phone's mouthpiece with one hand. "She wanted to know if you're free to see a movie. I told her you're too busy practicing for the big state competition." She beamed. "My little champion!"

Wendy grabbed the phone from her mom. "Sorry, Cassie. No time today. I've got gymnastics. The championships are in two weeks, and I still have a ton to do on my balance beam routine."

"This is like the third time I've asked you to do something and you couldn't go!" Cassie huffed on the other end.

"Can we talk about this later? I've gotta get going," Wendy replied.

"Whatever!" Cassie said. The phone went dead in Wendy's hand. She handed it back to her mom.

"How about some breakfast before you go? I have some scrambled eggs ready," her mom said.

"No time!" Wendy responded. "I'll grab something later. I can't be late for practice." I'm fat enough anyway, she thought.

Talk About It

- How do you think Cassie felt when she constantly got the brush-off from Wendy?

- Have you ever neglected your friends because you were so into one of your activities? How did your friends react?

- What might happen if Wendy continues to work at this pace?

Coach Jones was pointing to her watch when Wendy arrived ten minutes late. "Ladies, we need to be on time for these practices! Champions don't lag behind." Wendy mumbled a quick apology and ran over to the balance beam. She needed at least a few hours of practice today if she was going to perfect her routine.

Pirouette, handstand, back walkover to back handspring. Darn! She slipped again. Back up on the beam. Pirouette, handstand, back walkover. She was so off-balance this morning, and she felt a little dizzy. She tried again. Pirouette, handstand, back walkover, back handspring. Everything was getting blurry. Suddenly, the balance beam wasn't under her feet anymore.

Suddenly, the balance beam wasn't under her feet anymore.

Wendy's wrist made a loud crack as she hit the ground. Seemingly in slow motion, Wendy could see her coach and teammates turning to look at her, the shock registering on their faces. Wendy looked down at her swelling wrist. She knew it was broken. Her dreams of winning a gold medal at state were over.

Talk About It

- Was winning too important to Wendy? Why or why not?

- Have you ever wanted to win at a sport so badly that you neglected other areas of your life? What happened?

- How could Wendy have created more balance in her life? What do you do when you feel like one area of your life is getting out of control?

Playing a sport is wonderful for your physical and mental health. It can teach you valuable skills such as teamwork and discipline, and it can give your self-esteem a real boost. But putting too much emphasis on competition and winning can put an unhealthy amount of pressure and stress on you and your body. So many young athletes these days are pushing themselves so hard to stay competitive that sports are no longer fun for them. Instead, sports become an obsession.

Though your parents and coaches have the best intentions—they want to see you succeed—they can add to the pressure you're already feeling. That's why it's important to speak up when you feel like the pressure is getting too intense. It's more important for you to be a healthy, well-rounded person. That means having a balanced lifestyle that includes enough sleep, healthful eating habits, and a reasonable social life. You'll have plenty of opportunities to win in sports and in other activities in the years ahead.

Get Healthy

1. Avoid injuries by taking time to rest after workouts. If you do get injured, give your body time to heal. Remember, this is the only body you'll have, so take good care of it.

2. Make time to just be a kid and have fun. Hang out with your friends, go to the movies or the mall, or just sit and read a book you love.

3. Your parents and coaches should be encouraging you—not pressuring you. If your father is calling you aside and yelling at you after each missed play, or your coach is berating you for gaining weight, ask for help from another trusted adult.

4. You need lots of energy to play a sport, and that means eating at least three well-balanced meals during the day. If you ever find yourself skipping meals, throwing up after meals, or seriously cutting calories, you could be developing an eating disorder. See your doctor or a dietitian right away for help.

The Last Word from Stephanie

Sports are meant to be played. When sports become more work than fun, you're no longer playing. Many young athletes have literally made themselves sick trying to be the best. Famous gymnasts Kathy Johnson and Nadia Comaneci struggled with eating disorders. Tennis player Andrea Jaeger was so burned out by age 18 that she dropped out of the sport. Have fun in your sport, but be careful not to let the game take over your life.

7

The Poser

Everyone wants to fit in, feel included, and be liked. Being connected to others not only feels good, but studies have shown that people with close emotional ties to others lead healthier lives. Being part of a great group of girls can be an invaluable support in facing life's challenges.

Despite the benefits of close relationships, you have to choose your friends wisely. Some girls can be moody or inconsiderate. They can be fake or fickle or talk behind your back. Other girls can be the most loving, caring, supportive friends ever! It's up to you to connect with caring people and together create positive, healthy relationships.

Friendships can teach us valuable lessons about getting along with others. You need to know how to be a good friend. You also need to know how to maintain your own identity, use your own judgment, and not get so over-involved in your group that you base your identity on being accepted or popular. Read on to learn how Alyssa made that mistake and what it cost her.

Alyssa's Story

Alyssa peeked through the window of the science lab door, hoping for a glimpse of *him*. Her heart leapt when she saw him.

Quickly, she leaned back against the wall so Toby wouldn't catch her staring at him. Her heart was racing and her palms were sweaty.

Alyssa peeked through the window of the science lab door, hoping for a glimpse of *him*. Her heart leapt when she saw him.

Straightening up, she smoothed her hair and adjusted her sweatshirt. I'm cool . . . he has no clue I like him . . . no one does, she thought to herself. Nervously she looked down the hallway to make sure that Mary and Suzanne weren't back from lunch yet. They always hung out to talk to the eighth grade boys, so Alyssa knew she had a few minutes.

Alyssa tried to appear nonchalant as she opened the science room door and went to her seat by the front. Toby got up from his seat in the back by the window. Alyssa pretended not to notice him.

Talk About It

- Why do you think Alyssa is so nervous to see Toby? Why does she pretend not to notice him when he gets up from his seat?

- Why do you think Alyssa wanted to make sure that Mary and Suzanne weren't back from lunch yet?

Toby stood by her desk wearing jeans and a T-shirt covered in electric guitars and skulls. The T-shirt was the exact same color as his dreamy blue eyes. "Hi, Alyssa," he said.

She looked up. "Oh, hey."

"I wanted to show you my latest sketch." He slipped a piece of paper onto her desk. It was a take on Wonder Woman, but she had flames for hair and lightning bolts in her hands. Alyssa loved how powerful he'd made the woman look and how perfectly he'd drawn the flames in her hair. Alyssa thought it was awesome.

Suddenly Mary and Suzanne came over and Mary grabbed the sketch. "Like cartoons much? Are you in like, first grade?" Alyssa's cheeks reddened as her best friends laughed.

Toby grabbed for the sketch. "Hey! Give it back! It's for Alyssa!"

Mary dropped the paper on the floor. "Alyssa doesn't want your stupid cartoons."

"Yeah, she doesn't like *little* boys like you," Suzanne scoffed.

"Seventh grade boys are losers," Mary taunted. "Isn't that right, Alyssa?"

Talk About It

- Should Alyssa say anything to her friends? If so, what should she say?

- Have you ever felt embarrassed or uncomfortable with a friend's behavior? If so, what did you do?

Alyssa wanted to sink into a hole and die. But no escape was going to magically appear in science lab. Alyssa had been best friends with Mary and Suzanne since fourth grade. Her friends were her entire world. If they didn't like Toby, there was no way she was going to get away with even talking to him. They were especially particular about who was cool and who was a loser. If Alyssa hung out with a loser, then her friends might consider *her* a loser. Then where would she be?

Swallowing, Alyssa shrugged. "Ah, yeah, cartoons are a bit juvenile." Toby angrily picked up the sketch and headed to the back of the class. Alyssa's heart sank as she watched him go.

Talk About It

- **How do you think Alyssa felt about herself when she made fun of Toby's sketch?**

- **What do you think Mary and Suzanne would've done if Alyssa had defended Toby?**

- **What do you think would happen if Alyssa admitted to her friends that she liked Toby?**

After class, Alyssa kept her head down as she walked out of science lab with her friends. She didn't want to see Toby with her friends nearby. As usual, the girls went straight to the fourth floor stairwell, where they would meet up with the eighth grade boys. Alyssa didn't like the eighth graders; they made her feel young and a little stupid. They made inside jokes that she didn't catch. But Mary and Suzanne loved the eighth graders. They said that it made them cool to hang with the older boys.

Tommy Dawson, an eighth grader who Mary thought was cute, mentioned that he wouldn't mind hanging out the upcoming weekend. Mary immediately volunteered that Alyssa's parents would be gone on Friday night, so they could meet at Alyssa's house.

Alyssa was mortified. She didn't want the eighth graders at her house. More importantly, her parents would kill her if she had boys over when they were gone! On the way to class, Alyssa tried to talk to her friends about it, but they didn't care. All they thought about was being with the eighth grade boys. Alyssa began to wonder if her friends cared about her at all.

Talk About It

- Have you ever followed someone else's plans, even when you knew they weren't right? Why did you do that?

- Have you ever felt like you were doing things just to fit in?

- What might happen if Alyssa doesn't go along with Mary and Suzanne's plan for the weekend? What would you do?

Later that day, Alyssa found Toby hanging out with his friends by his locker. Slowly she approached. "Hey, Toby," she said timidly.

Later that day, Alyssa found Toby hanging out with his friends by his locker. Slowly she approached.

Toby's gorgeous blue eyes narrowed, but he jerked his chin in response. "Hey."

Alyssa shifted her weight. "I'm, ah, sorry about my friends. I really did like your sketch."

Toby shook his head. "If you had told me that in class it would've made my day. But now, I can't be friends with you, Alyssa."

Her eyes widened. "But I didn't mean what I said—"

Toby turned away. "I can't be friends with someone who can't think for herself. See ya around."

Talk About It

- Was Toby too harsh to say that he couldn't be friends with Alyssa? Why or why not?

- How do you think Alyssa felt to hear Toby's comments? Do you think she'll change who she hangs out with?

- Have you ever ended a friendship with someone because of something they said or did? What happened?

Going along with others to be accepted or popular isn't being honest with yourself or with your friends. How can you form a real connection with someone if you don't let them know who you really are? Try to keep in mind that everyone has something to offer. You need to recognize your own beauty and strength and be true to your values. Be willing to take the risk to say what's on your mind. Even if it isn't received well, at least you'll be able to walk away knowing that what you did was right.

Try not to allow yourself to be influenced by others, especially if it goes against your own judgment. Be nice to everyone, but try to avoid girls who are mean, cliquey, or a bad influence. You can make smart choices about who you want to be and who you want around you. Choose your friends wisely and be the kind of friend you want to have. If you value loyalty, then be loyal. If you want friends who cheer you on, be supportive to them. If you want your friends to be straight with you, be honest with them. Your sincere friendship may inspire others to reach their own potential.

Get Healthy

1. Choose friends who are supportive of who you are now and who encourage you in positive ways.

2. Be a caring, trustworthy friend to others and it will attract good friends to you.

3. Have friends in diverse areas of your life such as at school, in sports, and in your religious institution. Having different groups of friends will give you a broad support system.

4. Be kind to everyone. You never know who will turn out to be a good friend or when you may need a new friend.

The Last Word from Sari

When I was in seventh grade, I was assigned to a different class from my best friends. At first, I was crushed. But then I realized I needed to make friends in my own class or I was going to have a very lonely year. So I invited girls I didn't know so well over to my house for a class project. One of those girls was named Bonnie. She wasn't the most popular girl in the class, but she was really kind and friendly. Bonnie and I became best friends. Since then she's helped me get through some of the toughest times in my life and shared some of my happiest moments. So remember to be yourself and don't overlook the girl sitting next to you—she might turn out to be a truly wonderful friend.

8

The Failing Student

The teacher's pet—just about every class has one. She's the one who gets straight As, answers every question correctly, and can do no wrong in her teacher's eyes.

But for every teacher's pet there is at least one student who can't seem to do anything right. The failing students barely squeak by on tests and never seem to know the answer. Sometimes these students don't try at all, and sometimes they try hard but just can't seem to find success.

Teachers work very hard to make sure that all of their students learn, but they also face pressures— from the principal, parents, and the school board—to produce good grades. Sometimes teachers pass these pressures on to their students, especially the struggling ones. Erin is one of these students. Her teacher came down hard on her day after day, until Erin reached the breaking point.

Erin's Story

"The innermost part of Earth is called what? Erin?" Miss Phillips motioned toward Erin, who was slumped as far down into her seat as she could get without falling on the floor.

Erin looked at her teacher blankly. How the heck should I know? she thought. "Ummm, magma?" she said.

"This was in last night's reading homework, Erin. There's no reason for you not to know the answer," Miss Phillips scolded. "Please see me after class. We have a test on Friday, and you need to be ready. All of you need to be ready. I can't continue to see failing grades."

"This was in last night's reading homework, Erin. There's no reason for you not to know the answer," Miss Phillips scolded.

Everyone turned to look at Erin. She stared at her shoes, embarrassed and wondering if everyone in her class hated her.

Talk About It

- **Have you ever been called on in class and not known the answer? How did you feel?**

- **Do you think that Miss Phillips was too hard on Erin? Do you think Miss Phillips cares about her students?**

When she shuffled her way to her teacher's desk after class, Erin knew what to expect. This was the fourth time in a week she'd gotten in trouble for not knowing the answer. Miss Phillips had her head in her hands. She looked as though she had a terrible headache. "Erin, did you bother to read the material last night?" Miss Phillips sighed.

"I—I did read it. I just didn't get it," Erin stammered.

"Really, Erin. This isn't difficult work." Miss Phillips looked at her pointedly. "I know you're a bright girl. If you'd just apply yourself, I'm sure you could do really well. If you don't bring up these grades, you're looking at repeating my class next year."

Erin's cheeks turned red. Repeat science with Miss Phillips? She'd rather go to the dentist and have her teeth drilled every day.

Talk About It

- Do you think Erin is really slacking off, or just having trouble understanding the material?

- Have you ever had a teacher single you out to tell you that you need to improve your grade? What happened and how did it make you feel?

"I can't stand Miss Phillips!" Erin announced as she slammed her locker closed.

Her friend Amy nodded in agreement. "Yeah, she's a total pain."

"She's always picking on me, and she makes me feel like an idiot," Erin continued as they started to walk down the hall to the cafeteria for lunch. "You know, I wish there were some way to get back at her for always embarrassing me."

"Maybe she has some terrible family secret you could reveal," Amy chuckled.

"That would be nice." Erin smiled. "Or, maybe I just need to get a backbone. You know, confront her.

Tell her she's being too hard on me." She thought for a few seconds. "Go ahead to the cafeteria without me. I'll meet you after school."

Before Amy had a chance to respond, Erin was already striding down the hallway in the direction of Miss Phillips's classroom. When she got to Miss Phillips's door, ready to state her case, she noticed that someone was already in there. It was Principal Jackson. Erin didn't mean to eavesdrop, but she couldn't help but hear the loud conversation coming from inside the classroom.

"You don't seem to understand, Miss Phillips," Principal Jackson was saying in a condescending voice. "If we don't bring up our grades quickly, we're going to take a real funding hit, and the school board's going to have it out for me."

"I *do* understand, Principal Jackson. I'm doing everything I can to improve our grades. These are good kids—smart kids. I'm trying to help them excel, but I have no time or resources to work with," Miss Phillips responded. Her voice sounded tired.

"Well you're go-ing to need to work some magic, because if *my* job's in trouble, we're *all* in trouble. Be ready to report this semester's test scores at our meeting next Friday." With that, he walked out of the room.

Talk About It

- **What kind of pressures do you think your teachers face?**

- **Do you think overhearing the conversation between Miss Phillips and Principal Jackson will change how Erin feels about her teacher?**

Erin stood outside the door. She'd been so worried about the pressures Miss Phillips was putting on her that she'd never stopped to wonder whether her teacher had pressures of her own.

Then suddenly, Miss Phillips was at the door. "Erin—what are you doing here?" She looked startled, and her eyes were red, as though she'd been crying.

Erin had prepared a speech about how Miss Phillips was treating her unfairly, but how could she complain after what she'd just heard? Instead she said, "I just wanted you to know that I'm going to work much harder to improve my grades. I'm sorry I've been such a difficult student."

Miss Phillips softened. "Oh, Erin. I'm sorry I've been so hard on you. It's just that I've been under a lot of pressure, and I've had so little time to work with my students individually. I should have helped you if you were struggling. Why don't we talk to your guidance counselor and parents, and see if we can work together to improve your grades?"

Erin felt relieved. "That would be great," she said. "Then you'll be under less pressure because the class grades will go up."

Miss Phillips shook her head. "This isn't about me—it's about you," she said. "I want to see *you* succeed."

Talk About It

- **What are some ways that Erin could improve her grades?**

- **How did hearing about the pressure on Miss Phillips change Erin's perspective about her teacher?**

Girls struggle in school for many reasons. They might have a learning disability, such as dyslexia, that makes it difficult to read, write, or solve math problems. Some people have different learning styles or just learn better in smaller classes. Some girls who are very smart actually try not to get good grades because they're afraid it will make them unpopular. They worry that they'll be teased and labeled a teacher's pet or a nerd.

If your teacher seems to be too hard on you, don't assume it's because she dislikes you or thinks you're stupid. She may be singling you out because she really believes in you and thinks you can accomplish more than you are. If you're really struggling and your teacher isn't helping, talk to your parents, guidance counselor, or principal. Ask them to intervene, and see if you can get some extra help to improve your grades.

Get Healthy

1. If your teacher is giving you a hard time, find out why. Set up a meeting to talk to her in private and respectfully explain how you feel. If your teacher comes down harder on you for speaking up, it's time to enlist the help of your guidance counselor and parents.

2. To help you succeed in school, stay organized. Make "to do" lists of homework assignments and upcoming tests, and check off each item as you complete it.

3. Get a study buddy. Find someone you work well with to help you get ready for assignments and tests.

4. Don't be too hard on yourself. Just because you're struggling in school doesn't mean you're stupid. Praise yourself for the things you do right, and get help in the areas where you're having difficulty.

The Last Word from Stephanie

Your school years will be filled with highs and lows—great achievements, and at least a few disappointments. You'll undoubtedly face a lot of pressure, not only from your teachers, but also from your peers, parents, and eventually college admissions staff. If you're struggling in school and feeling stressed out as a result, don't be afraid to ask for help. Your parents and guidance counselor can arrange for tutoring or other extra assistance. Once you get the help you need, school will be a lot easier and a lot less stressful.

9

Miss Do-It-All

*L*ife can be really hectic. Between homework, tests, extracurricular activities, and a decent social life, it can feel as if there aren't enough hours in the day to do everything you want to do. On top of it all, you want a little time for yourself too.

Some girls love being busy. They live for trying new activities, getting really good at a favorite sport, or working hard and doing terrific in school. This kind of passion can be really healthy and lead to great success in life. These extra efforts can also be rewarding and lead to a greater sense of confidence.

If the pressure to achieve becomes overwhelming, though, it can work against you. Read Elizabeth's story to learn how she took on too much. Putting too much pressure on herself put everything she worked for at risk.

Elizabeth's Story

Elizabeth stared at the research paper in her hand, unwilling to believe it. She'd gotten a B-minus. She rubbed her eyes to make sure she wasn't seeing things. This was impossible. In her entire student life, from elementary school through seventh grade, she'd never made below an A.

Elizabeth lived by the code that success was based on achieving perfect grades and excellent scores, and being the best at

This was impossible. In her entire student life, from elementary school through seventh grade, she'd never made below an A.

everything she did. She had decided that there was little room for second best unless it was someone else. She made straight As, participated in a host of extra-curricular activities, and was a favorite of every teacher she'd ever had. No, this had to be a mistake.

Elizabeth approached her teacher's desk. "Ah, Ms. Dempsey? There seems to be a mistake with my paper. It says B-minus, and I know that this paper was A-plus material. It needs correction."

Ms. Dempsey looked up from her papers. "Are you grading me, now, Elizabeth?" Elizabeth opened her mouth and then closed it. Idiot! Elizabeth chided herself in her head. She should have asked for feedback, and flattered her teacher a bit. Now she'd be stuck with this crummy grade forever!

Talk About It

- Do you ever call yourself names inside your head? Are they kind and supportive or negative and cruel?

- Have you ever thought you'd done great on a test or paper only to find that you hadn't? If so, what did you do?

- What do you think of Elizabeth's comments to Ms. Dempsey about her grade?

Elizabeth stood before Ms. Dempsey and pasted on a smile. "I really did try, Ms. Dempsey, and I know that the work is solid material." Solid A material, she added in her head hopefully.

Ms. Dempsey frowned. "I disagree. The research was shallow. You didn't dig deep enough, and as a consequence your conclusions were weak. If I didn't know any better, I'd say that you tried to coast on this one, Elizabeth."

Elizabeth was shocked. Well, maybe she had tried to coast a bit, but it had been a crazy week with soccer drills, practice for the flute recital, and Dylan's party last weekend. I'm an idiot! Elizabeth screamed in her

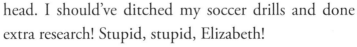

head. I should've ditched my soccer drills and done extra research! Stupid, stupid, Elizabeth!

At the look on Elizabeth's face, Ms. Dempsey added, "Don't worry, Elizabeth, you'll have a chance to pull up your grade with the final research paper due in two weeks."

Elizabeth left the classroom and headed to her locker, her mind racing. Two weeks? She had her flute recital coming up and the soccer tournament next week, not to mention that she was on the committees for decorations and entertainment for the big dance at the end of the month. Then Mr. Cooper was giving a math exam on Friday, and Mrs. Linowes always gave pop quizzes at the end of the unit. How was she going to write a research paper with that kind of crazy schedule?

Her heart was racing, her palms were sweating, and panic rose up in her stomach. She felt like she was going to throw up.

Talk About It

- Have you ever felt overwhelmed by too many demands on your time?

- Do you think Elizabeth can handle all of her homework and activities?

- Do you ever feel overscheduled? If so, what do you do about it?

Two weeks later, Elizabeth was a walking train wreck. She'd had four hours of sleep in two days and had been living on diet soda and jellybeans. Also, she'd missed the soccer team party, and her teammates were ticked. Still, she'd gotten the research paper done and knew it was good. But was it too good? Elizabeth had felt so pressured to get an A on her research paper that she'd copied quite a bit from an article she'd found on the Internet. She did try to change a word here and there, but all of the conclusions were from that article. Plus, when it had come time for the bibliography, Elizabeth had fudged quite a bit.

Later that day, Elizabeth got home from school and crashed onto her bed. She didn't have the energy to lift her backpack, let alone take out her textbooks and do her homework. Her phone rang, but she ignored it. Her mother called to her from downstairs, but she was too tired to respond. She felt like she could sleep forever, if only her head wasn't killing her. She felt as if someone was cutting her head in half with an ax, and she was freezing cold. She peeked at the clock. 5:15 p.m. Oh no! she thought. Dance committee meeting starts in 15 minutes!

Elizabeth's body hurt so much she wanted to cry. Still, she pushed herself up out of bed. Her mother came into the bedroom carrying a piece of paper in her hand. "Elizabeth, I got the most troubling e-mail from Ms. Dempsey," she said. "She wants to meet with your father and me after school tomorrow. Something about plagiarism."

Elizabeth's body hurt so much she wanted to cry. Still, she pushed herself up out of bed.

Elizabeth's mom looked at her daughter. "Elizabeth! You look terrible! Are you sick?" Her mother pressed her hand to Elizabeth's forehead.

Standing, Elizabeth brushed off her mother's hand. "I'm fine . . . gotta get to school . . . can't be late for the meeting . . . " Then she fell to the floor.

Talk About It

- How did Elizabeth make herself so ill?

- Have you ever felt pressured to take a shortcut in your schoolwork? What was it, and what happened in the end?

- How do you think Elizabeth's actions will affect her grades? How will her actions affect what her parents and teachers think about her?

Ask Dr. Robyn

We're each a work-in-progress, and our priorities shift and change as we grow. But if you don't take care of yourself, you won't be able to accomplish everything on your list. The pressure to take on "everything" has to be balanced with a healthy lifestyle, or it can lead to mental, physical, emotional, or social problems. Are you skipping meals because life's too packed? Are you getting enough sleep? Are you avoiding friends because you feel so overwhelmed that you don't have time to socialize? If you're so tired you can't function, then something needs to give.

If you're feeling overwhelmed, you need to get help. Talk to a supportive parent, counselor, or family member who can help you craft a workable schedule. Or if you're feeling really anxious, get professional counseling. Try to keep in mind that you don't have to do it all perfectly, and you don't have to do it all alone.

Get Healthy

1. Use a calendar to map out your activities. When you're considering signing up for something, you can make sure that you don't have any conflicts.

2. When organizing your time, be sure to remember that your health and well-being

must be central to everything you do. Make sure you have enough time for sleep, exercise, social interaction—and don't forget about fun!

3. If you feel overwhelmed, talk to a compassionate listener, such as a parent, a school counselor, or a teacher. That person can work with you to lighten your load. Remember, you don't have to do it all. It's okay to say no!

The Last Word from Sari

I had the opportunity once to hear a great educator speak to a class that was starting middle school. Instead of a long speech about overcoming challenges or being the best, the speaker surprised me. He advised the students to prioritize their goals and to not take on too much. They should focus on a few things they are passionate about. His words made me examine my own academic path. Looking back, I wish that I'd done more activities that were personally fulfilling to me, such as taking writing classes or being more involved in my community. It's taken me years to realize that it's not just about the grade, the score, or being the best, but it's really about enjoying the journey to get there. And the same is true for you.

A Second Look

Whether we like it or not, stress is a natural part of life. Pressure is part of what helps us survive and succeed. Humans have what's called "the stress response," also known as "fight or flight." These days, for the most part, stresses are less obvious and more long-term than they have been in the past. So our bodies need to learn how to deal with a different kind of pressure—pressure that's prolonged and from various sources.

Balancing stress is one of those worthwhile efforts that will always be a work-in-progress. Some people are better at dealing with pressure than others, and some people never quite get the hang of it. Even though we are adults, we are still learning to deal with the various pressures in our lives and trying to forgive ourselves when we don't get things just right.

The goal, in the end, is trying to lead a healthy life. A critical factor is balancing pressure so that it's positive and not overwhelming. This kind of balance requires that you take care of yourself and your body. For your body you need to eat right, get enough sleep, exercise to relieve stress, and never ever do anything to hurt yourself. For your emotional well-being, you need to try to keep yourself away from people who pressure you in negative ways or who aren't good influences on you. Additionally, you need to give yourself the love and support you would give your closest friend. Take care, and have fun!

XOXO,
Sari and Stephanie

Pay It Forward

Remember, a healthful life is about balance. Now that you know how to walk that path, pay it forward to a friend or even to yourself! Remember the Get Healthy tips throughout this book, and then take these steps to get healthy and get going.

• Be honest with the people who are putting pressure on you, whether it's your parents, friends, teachers, or coaches. Let them know the stress is getting to be too much. If they can't help, talk to your school's guidance counselor, your doctor, or a therapist. Be specific about what you can handle and what kind of "coaching" works best for you.

• Start to become aware of the pressure you might be putting on others. Are you the "perfect" big sister with whom your little sibling just can't compete? Do you criticize your friends for weighing too much or wearing what you judge to be the wrong clothes? Always try to see the situation from the other person's perspective.

• Learn how to manage your time so that you don't become overwhelmed by school, homework, and other activities. Keep lists and schedules on a calendar, computer, or cell phone to help you stay organized.

- Exercise is a great way to relieve stress and stay healthy, but don't push yourself in any sport or activity that stresses you out too much. Instead, participate in activities that are fun and build up your self-esteem.

- Always make time for yourself. Whether you like to go to the movies, listen to music, or just curl up with a great book, make sure you build enough time into each day for your favorite activities.

- Instead of looking up to the popular girls because they wear expensive clothes, or to celebrities because they're rich and beautiful, find real sources of inspiration in your life— such as your teachers, siblings, and parents.

- Keep in mind all of the wonderful things that make you special. Sometimes it helps to write down all your talents and skills, and take out the list whenever you're starting to feel down on yourself.

- Surround yourself with people who build you up, rather than bring you down. Your friends should support you and be there when you need them. They should never criticize you or make you feel like you're not important. And they should absolutely never bully or victimize you.

- If your stress is due to any type of abuse— physical, sexual, or emotional—get help from a parent or health professional immediately.

Additional Resources

Select Bibliography

Covey, Sean. *The 7 Habits of Highly Effective Teens.* New York: Fireside, 1998.

Karres, Erika V. Shearin. *Mean Chicks, Cliques, and Dirty Tricks: A Real Girl's Guide to Getting Through the Day With Smarts and Style.* Avon, MA: Adams Media, 2004.

Muharrar, Aisha. *More Than a Label: Why What You Wear or Who You're With Doesn't Define Who You Are.* Minneapolis, MN: Free Spirit Publishing, 2002.

Pipher, Mary. *Reviving Ophelia: Saving the Selves of Adolescent Girls.* New York: Putnam, 1994.

Stenson, Jacqueline. "Pushing Too Hard Too Young." *MSNBC.* 29 Apr. 2004. <http://www.msnbc.msn.com/id/4556235/>.

Further Reading

Beck, Debra, and Maggie Anthony. *My Feet Aren't Ugly!: A Girl's Guide to Loving Herself From the Inside Out.* New York: Beaufort Books, 2007.

Carnegie, Donna Dale. *How To Win Friends and Influence People for Teen Girls.* New York: Simon & Schuster, 2005.

Macavinta, Courtney, and Andrea Vander Pluym. *Respect: A Girl's Guide to Getting Respect & Dealing When Your Line Is Crossed.* Minneapolis, MN: Free Spirit Publishing, 2005.

Weston, Carol. *Girltalk: All The Stuff Your Sister Never Told You.* New York: HarperPerennial, 2004.

Web Sites

To learn more about coping with pressure, visit ABDO Publishing Company online at **www.abdopublishing.com**. Web sites about coping with pressure are featured on our Book Links page. These links are routinely monitored and updated to provide the most current information available.

For More Information

For more information on this subject, contact or visit the following organizations.

About Face

P.O. Box 77665, San Francisco, CA 94107
415-436-0212
www.about-face.org
About Face works to stop negative media images that can damage girls' self-esteem.

Girls for a Change

P.O. Box 1436, San Jose, CA 95109
408-540-6432
www.girlsforachange.org
This organization empowers girls to be forces for social change and offers them inspiring female role models.

Girls Inc.

120 Wall Street, New York, NY 10005-3902
212-509-2000
www.girlsinc.org
Girls Inc. is an organization that addresses the social, educational, and emotional issues facing young girls today.

Glossary

berate
> To scold or lecture someone.

clique
> A group of friends who share the same interests and types of behavior.

computation
> A math calculation.

condescending
> Treating a person as if he or she is beneath you.

dyslexia
> A learning disability that makes it difficult to read and write.

emulate
> To copy or imitate someone you admire.

external
> Outside.

extracurricular
> Athletic and social activities that occur outside of school.

inaudible

Too low in volume to hear.

insecurity

Lacking in self-confidence.

kleptomania

A continuous abnormal desire to steal.

mediator

Someone who helps resolve differences between people.

overbearing

Overly bossy.

plagiarism

The act of copying someone else's work and presenting it as your own (such as a term paper).

scrimmage

A practice game, such as in soccer.

Index

About the Authors

Sari Earl is an attorney. After winning first place in a writing competition, she began a full-time writing career. She's gone on to write several novels of adult fiction, which have been published in countries around the world. Sari loves to write. In addition to novels, she's written articles and young adult books. She lives in Atlanta, Georgia, with her family.

Stephanie Watson is a freelance writer based in Atlanta, Georgia. Over the years she has written for television, radio, the Internet, and print. Her books include *Daniel Radcliffe, Understanding Obesity: The Genetics of Obesity, What's in Your Food? Recipe for Disaster: Fast Food*, and *Living Green: Recycling*. She has been nominated for a National Online Journalism award and has won a PROMAX Silver award for television promotion.

Photo Credits

David Davis/Fotolia, 12; Fotolia, 14, 18, 64, 69, 76; Michael Drager/Fotolia, 25; Luis Sierra/iStockphoto, 27; Jules Studio/Shutterstock Images, 29; Michael Chamberlin/Fotolia, 35; Amy Myers/Fotolia, 39; Galina Barskaya/Fotolia, 45; Rich Legg/iStockphoto, 49; Wendy Nero/Shutterstock Images, 54; Bonnie Schupp/iStockphoto, 56; iStockphoto, 66; Lorraine Swanson/Fotolia, 75; Elena Elisseeva/Shutterstock Images, 84; Eric Hood/iStockphoto, 86; Monkey Business/Fotolia, 89; Laurence Gough/Shutterstock Images, 95; Tracy Martinez/Fotolia, 96; Miramiska/Shutterstock Images, 99